Good Manners on the Phone

May I ask who is calling?

by Katie Marsico
illustrated by John Haslam
Content consultant: Robin Gaines Lanzi, PhD, MPH,
Department of Human Science, Georgetown University

visit us at www.abdopublishing.com

Published by Magic Wagon, a division of the ABDO Group, 8000 West 78th Street, Edina, Minnesota, 55439. Copyright © 2009 by Abdo Consulting Group, Inc. International copyrights reserved in all countries. All rights reserved. No part of this book may be reproduced in any form without written permission from the publisher.

Looking Glass Library™ is a trademark and logo of Magic Wagon.

Printed in the United States.

Text by Katie Marsico
Illustrations by John Haslam
Edited by Amy Van Zee
Interior layout and design by Becky Daum
Cover design by Becky Daum

Library of Congress Cataloging-in-Publication Data
Marsico, Katie, 1980-
  Good manners on the phone / by Katie Marsico ; illustrated by John Haslam.
      p. cm. — (Good manners matter!)
  Includes bibliographical references (p.   ).
  ISBN 978-1-60270-611-8
  1. Telephone etiquette—Juvenile literature. I. Haslam, John. II. Title.
  BJ2195.M37 2009
  395.5—dc22

                                    2008036323

Contents

Why Do Good Manners Matter on the Phone?

You hear the phone ring and you race to answer it. The caller is looking for your sister. You don't know if she is home. Should you order the caller to wait while you scream your sister's name?

You might already know that it isn't good manners to shout into the phone. It's polite to ask the caller to please hold. Then, look for the person he or she is calling for. Do you know why good manners matter on the phone?

Good manners are about thinking of others, not just yourself. Being polite to others lets them know that you value and respect them.

Imagine talking on the phone if no one had good manners. People might hang up on each other all the time. They would shout into the phone. People might not take messages. You would never know if your best friend called while you were out.

You wouldn't enjoy talking on the phone if people were this rude. How can you practice good manners when you talk on the phone?

Show Good Manners on the Phone!

Sometimes people call you. Other times you might call them. You should be polite in both situations. It's important to show respect for anyone on the other end of the line. Give that person your full attention.

Be sure you are in a quiet room when you talk on the phone. Turn off the television or the radio. It will then be easier for both of you to hear each other.

How should you speak when someone calls your house? Start by greeting them with "hello" in a clear voice. Then let the caller tell you his or her name and who they want to reach.

What happens if the caller doesn't tell you this information? Next say, "May I ask who is calling?" Ask the caller to please hold while you see if that person can come to the phone.

Always put the phone down when checking if someone can come to the phone. Never shout while the caller is waiting. Yelling is rude and will hurt the caller's ears. Perhaps the person the caller is looking for is in another part of your house. Once you find him or her, explain who is calling.

If your parents are gone and a person calls for them, don't tell the caller they are gone. Talk to your parents about what they would like you to say if this happens. You could tell the caller that your mom or dad can't come to the phone.

If someone can't come to the phone, offer to take a message. Use neat handwriting when you note the caller's information. You might ask for their phone number or how to spell their name. Sometimes the person may tell you why they're calling.

Be sure to give the message to the person it is meant for. Or, leave it in a spot where the person is certain to find it. Don't forget to say "good-bye" in a clear voice when the phone call is over!

Of course, you don't have to wait for a call to talk on the phone. You can still practice good manners when you call another person. Suppose someone else answers the phone when you call your friend Annie's house. First, introduce yourself. Then, simply say, "May I please speak to Annie?" Ask if you can leave a message if she isn't home.

It's good manners not to make phone calls during certain times of the day. Don't call too early in the morning or too late at night. Also, don't call when people may be eating meals.

Other words that show good manners on the phone are "thank you" and "you are welcome." You can practice good manners by saying these words any time you speak to someone else. Let's get ready to see some good manners in motion!

Manners in Motion

Juan turned down his radio when he heard the phone ring. He knew he couldn't hear the caller if loud music was playing.

"Hello," he said in a clear voice.

"Hello," the caller said back. "May I please speak to Gina?" Gina was Juan's younger sister.

"May I ask who is calling?" Juan replied.

"This is Mrs. Charles, Gina's piano teacher."

"Can you please hold for a moment?" Juan asked.
Mrs. Charles agreed to wait. Juan put the phone
down and knocked quietly on Gina's door. Then he
remembered she was at the park. He returned to the
phone.

"Gina can't come to the phone right now, Mrs. Charles. May I take a message?" Juan said.

"Yes, thank you," said Mrs. Charles.

"May I please have your phone number?" Juan asked. Mrs. Charles gave him the number. Juan carefully wrote it down. He also noted that it was 3:30 PM when she called. He and Mrs. Charles then said "good-bye" to each other and hung up.

Juan left the message on his sister's desk. He also planned to tell Gina about the call when she returned from the park.

Can you name all the different ways Juan and
Mrs. Charles practiced good manners on the phone?
Having good manners is easy! Just remember to
be polite and show respect for the person on the
other end of the line. What good manners have you
practiced on the phone lately?

Amazing Facts about Manners on the Phone

Did You Just Say "Hello"?

Most people in the United States say "hello" when answering the phone. You might use other words if you lived in another country. Kids in Germany answer the phone by speaking their last name. Some people in Eastern Europe say "ready." These greetings are different but are all examples of good manners!

Calling Cards

How would you have planned visits with your friends before the telephone was invented? You would have had to leave calling cards at their homes. These were written greetings that people dropped off at each other's houses. Until the early 1900s, the cards were a polite way of asking to be invited for a visit. After the phone became common in people's homes, it was much easier to simply make a call to see if it was all right to come over!

Top Five Tips for Good Manners on the Phone

1. Don't shout.
2. Give the person on the phone your full attention.
3. Speak clearly.
4. Offer to take a message.
5. Don't forget to say "please," "thank you," and "good-bye!"

Glossary

greeting—words you say when you meet or see someone.
information—facts.
message—a way to tell or show someone something.
polite—showing good manners by the way you act or speak.
respect—a sign that you care about people or things and want to treat them well.
rude—showing bad manners by the way you act or speak.
situation—the event of a certain moment.

Web Sites

To learn more about manners, visit ABDO Group online at **www.abdopublishing.com**. Web sites about manners are featured on our Book Links page. These links are routinely monitored and updated to provide the most current information available.

Index